To Be Opened After My Death

To Be Opened After My Death

Poems by

Midge Goldberg

© 2021 Midge Goldberg. All rights reserved.
This material may not be reproduced in any form, published,
reprinted, recorded, performed, broadcast,
rewritten or redistributed without
the explicit permission of Midge Goldberg.
All such actions are strictly prohibited by law.

Cover design by Shay Culligan and Ely Campeanu
Author photograph by Ely Campeanu

Library of Congress Control Number: 2021916498
ISBN: 978-1-954353-91-6

Kelsay Books
502 South 1040 East, A-119
American Fork, Utah 84003
Kelsaybooks.com

For Bob

Acknowledgments

My thanks to the following publications, where several of the poems in this collection have been accepted for publication:

100 Poems: The Romantics: "Tomorrow at Dawn" (translation)

Able Muse: "The Molt"

Alabama Literary Review: "Arroyo," "Bernadette, On Playing Dolly on Broadway," "Florida, but Inland," "Playing Along in Temple"

Better Than Starbucks: "Circling"

First Things: "The Doctor and the Patient in the Next Exam Bay," "Echoes," "Prop Tools," "Reading the Signs"

Good Fat: "Cutting the Mustard"

The Hopkins Review: "This Coffee Pot"

Journal for General Internal Medicine: "Dressed for the Party," "The March of Time," "Planning Ahead"

Light: "Brooklyn Personals," "Curiosity No Longer Sings Happy Birthday to Itself," "Edna SVM, On Wearing Her First Bikini," "Funeral Potatoes," "Heading Out," "Ice Tray," "Man of Steel," "Pharaoh's Daughter," "Recipe for Disaster," "SmartTales"

Lighten Up Online: "Cloud 9," "Gift Horse," "The Plant Speaks," "Russian 'Trolls' Disrupt Elections"

Literary Mama: "Milk"

Measure: "In the Attic," "Tennis Practice Against the Garage Door," "To Be Opened After My Death"

Mezzo Cammin: "The Baker," "The Bartender," "The Fire Tender," "The Florist," "The Piano Player"

Contents

Circling

In the Attic	15
Circling	16
Ice Tray	17
Tennis Practice Against the Garage Door	19
To Be Opened After My Death	20
This Coffee Pot	21
Directions	23
The Inn: *The Fire Tender*	24

The Fifth Wall

Pharaoh's Daughter	29
Gift Horse	30
Edna SVM, on Wearing Her First Bikini	31
Bernadette, on Playing Dolly on Broadway	32
Milk	34
Curiosity No Longer Sings Happy Birthday to Itself	35
Tomorrow at Dawn	37
The Plant Speaks	38
The Inn: *The Florist*	39

Playing Along

Florida, but Inland	43
SmartTales	44
Man of Steel	46
Russian "Trolls" Disrupt Elections	47
Brooklyn Personals	49
The Doctor and the Patient in the Next Exam Bay	50

Speed of Sound	51
Playing Along in Temple	52
The Inn: *The Piano Player*	53

Reading the Signs

Reading the Signs	57
Cloud 9	58
Funeral Potatoes	59
Recipe for Disaster	60
Planning Ahead	61
Heading Out	62
Dressed for the Party	63
Tomato Seedlings in the Window	64
The Inn: *The Bartender*	65

Contours

Contours	69
Prop Tools	70
The March of Time	71
Arroyo	72
The Molt	74
The Inn: *The Baker*	75
Echoes	78

Circling

In the Attic

I'm looking through some boxes in the attic—
the kids sent photos that I want to hang.
It's dusty, hot up here, so I'm ecstatic
to find a frame, but realize with a pang

it's Aunt Lucille and Uncle Bob. The fun
couple, the black sheep of the family,
Jewish and Catholic when that "wasn't done"—
two artists who loved cats and who liked me.

It hits me: no one misses them at all.
They had no kids, there are no siblings left.
After he died, alone, I got the call.
I look at them and try to feel bereft.

It's not a tragedy, but such a shame.
Both lovely people, but I need the frame.

Circling

The devil doesn't need to use the door.
The devil doesn't need to have a key.
He's inside, and you're lying on the floor.

"The devil? He's a kind of dinosaur—
extinct; a quaint, outdated enemy.
The devil doesn't need to use the door—

the devil isn't coming anymore."
That's easy to repeat until you see
he's inside, and you're lying on the floor.

No horns, no tail, he doesn't look how you're
expecting, doesn't spout hyperbole—
the devil doesn't need to. Use the door,

don't use the door, it's really you—you swore
you'd shut him out and make him let you be.
He's inside. You're lying. On the floor,

inside your brain, impossible to ignore,
one worn-out thought keeps circling endlessly.
The devil doesn't need to use the door.
He's inside, and you're lying on the floor.

Ice Tray

Out on the counter, tray
of empty spaces,

Ice angels,
sandbox crenellation mold,

Egg carton with a dozen
hollow places,

Each four-walled plastic womb
ready to hold

A single cell of water—
filled, they are

Promises only,
precursors that require

A balancing act, martinis
on a bar,

Until, shape-shifter,
O transmogrifier!

Nursery of ice,
of building blocks,

Square worlds created
out of hydrogen bonds,

A flagstone patio
of slippery rocks,

Small skating rinks
on tiny frozen ponds,

Glass houses each
entirely alone,

Tumbling together
into the unknown.

Tennis Practice Against the Garage Door

"Impossible to win against the wall,"
my son mutters. I hear the bounce and slam
as he goes on hitting the tennis ball,
its arc and dip and arc a sonogram
of will. The wall returns one down the line
straight back at him, or else, in wall-like folly,
ricochets one off its beveled design—
it's out of bounds, and so he wins that volley.
Battling for the point that wins the game,
he finally calls "ad in" against the door.
Gripping the racquet, he takes careful aim.
This is the moment he's been training for—
the beauty in tenacity and sweat,
the ace over the imaginary net.

To Be Opened After My Death

To all the women of my generation,

My dresses, hats, the gloves, the high-heeled shoes,
were always pinks and reds (though I liked blues)—
the color, they said, added animation.

They had me marry for my reputation—
I did, without an inkling I could choose.
There was one time, a Caribbean cruise…
I had to be a symbol for the nation.

But there's another tale I couldn't tell
of when I disappeared in the war years—
a combat signals unit, code name "Spouse."
We signalleers all listened in on hell—
I grew to dread those words, "Put on your ears."
It's time you knew.

                                Minerva ("Minnie") Mouse

This Coffee Pot

Dented old-fashioned version of a moka,
that I have carried house to house for years
without ever knowing how it worked—
aluminum, like from a hobo's campfire,
two halves, two handles, looks almost the same
upside-down as right-side up. I frown,
trying to remember San Donato,
the coffee pot there,

                and that first cool morning
I walked up to the village to buy coffee.
The clerk thought I was ordering a cup—
I tried to make myself be understood:
No, scusa, what I wanted was a "purse"
(because I had not learned the word for "bag"
yet on my CD, *Visit Italy*,
which clearly thought that I would shop for leather
before bulk beans). She warmed to me and, handing
over the bag of beans, she waved away
my *latte, latte* (a word I actually knew),
dismissed the box of milk I pointed at
and pulled out a container of fresh milk
from somewhere cold hidden beneath the counter.
She said a word which must have meant "it's fresh"
(following the theory people are
usually saying what you think they are).
It sounded like "fresh," and so I smiled at her,
and she smiled back and took the right amount
from coins in my outstretched hand. I went back home,
holding my purse of coffee (*borsa*, "purse,"
can sometimes mean "bag" too, I found out later)
and my fresh milk, back to that coffee pot,
which sat there, small, shiny, inscrutable,

not offering any help on what to do.
But a good guess, also a basic grasp
of physics, led me then

                and now, to add
water to the bottom of the moka,
coffee on top, knowing the two would somehow
meet, creating coffee, the way I'd met
that one Italian clerk and we'd made coffee
out of a leather purse and "fresh" and knowing
about wrong words and love we carry around
waiting to be understood anyway.

Directions

Paper Map

The map is blind to where you are.
Mountain, valley, center, edge,
you could be anywhere, your car
parked along this road, that ledge.

You have to find yourself. Recall
the many twists and turns you took,
the signs you barely saw. How small
you are on paper. Get out and look.

•

GPS

That's you, that dot, right in the middle,
not lost at all. *Wherever you go,
there you are.* Oh, maybe you fiddle
with routes, but you follow yourself. You know.

Mountains, rivers, towns slide on
and off this map of you, your glassed-
in world that needs no north, no dawn,
no nightfall. You steer safely past.

And then you get there, where it's clear
you've been all along. What you went through?
Pointless to care. It's always here,
it's always now, it's always you.

The Inn:
The Fire Tender

With seven sitting rooms, the restaurant,
the lounge and lobby, it's a full-time job.
Though they don't think so—I'm always sent outside
to park the cars or shovel days-old snow.

They don't see the art of building fires,
finding a careful balance—a crackling flame
with heat that doesn't overwhelm the room.
There's tinkering with the flues; on windy days
or very still, it takes a delicate touch.
And brushing ashes off the wooden floors
and rugs—have they forgotten 1980?

Then there's the trick of how to be a shadow,
tending the fires while not disturbing guests
or drawing the attention of the children,
who want to help, but they are not allowed.

The hearth pile, that's an art all to itself.
I always use "log-cabin" style—I like
the airy space inside the sturdy frame.
The first square on the floor's the most important,
with each log flat and dry and uniform—
any wobble will bring the whole thing down
eventually. The pile's the signature:
I can tell who's worked by how the wood
is stacked. Roberto uses "tic-tac-toe,"
where wood is laid in threes, first one way then
the other. Then there's Steve, who just makes rows.
That's fine if he made "bookends"—he doesn't, though.
The danger comes in moving one end piece—

the logs roll down, a clatter and a mess.
And guess who'll fix it—I just want it right.

Of course, it's hard work too—who do you think
hauls all that wood? They keep a shed out back
stocked from the woodlot (I've worked out there too).
Early mornings we can use the cart
and elevator, bringing logs to stock
the piles in every room. But during the day,
one armload at a time—more picturesque,
I think they think—then sweep up the debris.
I don't mind carrying but do mind skulking,
the faint embarrassment when cleaning up,
as if it's from a misbehaving dog.

Usually I try ignoring guests;
sometimes they look right through me, or, what's worse,
talk in that hearty tone, which lets me know
they've never built a fire in their lives,
or split and stacked a woodpile.
                            But other times
I see a couple gazing at the flames,
a child with a toy down on the rug,
or someone reading, curled up on the couch
alone, but warm.

The Fifth Wall

Pharaoh's Daughter

Pharaoh's daughter…made him her son. She named him Moses, explaining, "I drew him out of the water."
—Exodus 2:10

Really? I find a baby in the water?
I've got to know my father's killing Jews,
and then some girl appears (dutiful daughter?
loving sister?), there with helpful news—

she might just know a wet-nurse for the baby.
What am I? Awkward plot device? Convenient
miracle? Much later, they say maybe
it was an act of faith, and they are lenient,

marry me off, give me a name. Fuck you.
"Batyah, daughter of God.*"* I'm Moses's mother—
skinned knees, homework, and then one day he knew,
and left behind our life to lead another.

I always had a future and a past—
It's only God who made me seem half-assed.

Gift Horse

Cassandra, yes, you had it bad.
You spoke—they wouldn't listen. Sad.

But face it, most days back in Troy,
there was no tragic Grecian ploy—

how often was there news so dire
that made you preach without a choir?

Really, worse than prophecy,
is seeing possibility:

What if this or *why not* that,
each day requires a caveat,

or two, or three, a Hydra's head
that multiplies on going to bed.

Whenever there's a choice of curse,
to wonder, not to know, is worse—

you really are the lucky one,
knowing all things under the sun,

not always asking of the sky,
What if, why not, why, why, why, why?

Edna SVM, on Wearing Her First Bikini

Breasts are just breasts, you guys, like feet or ears,
a pair you're born with—well, this pair appears
later, not all that useful till we need them,
when babies come along, and we can feed them.

Otherwise, they're more like lottery tickets,
this one gets "flat," that one gets "house of brick"—it's
just like you, with parts that vary in size,
but out of sight where we can't scrutinize.

We shouldn't let it be the start of wars—
it's out of our control, but out of yours,
I guess, a quick reaction you can't stifle
when, on a beach, you're greeted with an eyeful.

But size, just keep in mind while you are peeking,
is idle, biologically speaking.

Bernadette, on Playing Dolly on Broadway

So, sometimes I can't hit the highest notes.
That campy bit, pretending that I'm tired?
Yeah, sometimes I just need to catch my breath.
You'd never recognize this "Broadway star"
at ten a.m., hobbling around the room,
needing an hour to stand up, hit the john—
72 ain't 50, that's for sure.
Just think about your mother—who am I kidding,
your grandma doing shows six nights a week,
and twice on weekends. So yes, a dramatic pause…
can mean I'm pooped.
                    At noon, I take my limo
(though it's fun to think about the subway—
I'd wear a polyester jogging suit
and scarf and look like any other nonna)
and head down to the theater to get ready.
It takes a while to make me look this good.
But then it's time.
               I ride on stage—that bit
with a horse—and then you finally notice me.
I have to stand there casually while you clap,
a minute, more—my hand raised in a wave.
Sometimes just for fun I'll wink at you,
so you know that I know you know it's me,
we're in on this—this thing, this show—together.
I guess that's one thing age can let me do,
own everything: the stage, the seats, the story,
the fourth wall too.
                  And what about the ghosts?
Carol, Ethel, Barbra, they're all here,
we all hear them. We bring our ghosts as well,
whoever played the record for us first.
The house I play to has a fifth wall, time,

and all the seats are taken every night—
I've found that ghosts can be the toughest critics.

So I'll just break the wall because I can
and play for laughs to get you on my side,
ignoring my creaks and quavers. The cast is young;
I need you folks for company—we prop
each other up, whisper forgotten lines.
While everyone's together in this room,
we clap and laugh and cry and mug and sing—
we know we'll be alone when the curtain falls.

Milk

"That blanket's never going to give you milk,"
I tell the cat crossly,
watching him try to nurse.
I don't know why I'm angry
with the cat
except for the utter futility
of trying to get what you need
years too late
from something that bears
only the slightest resemblance
to a real mother
but you'd rather
suck a blanket
than know you'll never get
the milk you need.

Curiosity No Longer Sings Happy Birthday to Itself

"In a nutshell, there is no scientific gain from the rover playing music or singing 'Happy Birthday' on Mars," Tan said. In the battle between song and science, science always wins.
—The Atlantic

One year, in August, out in space,
dear Curiosity,
you slowed your point-oh-nine-mile pace,
and tuned yourself to C.

You answered the R.S.V.P.
programmed back on Earth,
played "Happy Birthday" wordlessly
to celebrate your birth.

So many million miles away
you hummed those sixteen bars,
wishing yourself a happy day
all alone on Mars.

And we all cried, "Oh, do not cry,
how lonely you must be,"
a party of one to satisfy
our curiosity.

Yes, of course we were aware
the loneliness was ours,
as we imagined being there,
all alone on Mars.

But still I pitied the ordeal
your code was going through—
not to think that you can feel
would mean I feel less too.

So sing again your silly song,
your birthday gift to me,
and I will cry and sing along,
unscientifically.

Tomorrow at Dawn

At dawn tomorrow, when the land turns white,
I'll leave, because I know you wait for me.
I'll go through forests, up the mountain's height.
I cannot stay away from you. I'll see

Nothing, my eyes fixed on my thoughts, alone,
And hear nothing, not a single sound or sight.
With my back bent, hands crossed, I'll walk, unknown,
Sad, and day for me will be like night.

I will not see the golden end of day,
Nor sails descend to Harfleur far away.
When I arrive, I'll put this on your tomb—
A bunch of holly sprigs, heather in bloom.

(translated from the French of Victor Hugo)

The Plant Speaks

I've grown up an ungrounded sort,
a hydroponic soul,
needing just a little water
and a hanging bowl.

My roots contained in one small ball,
I scorn the garden plot,
with no desire for floor space, just
a mid-air sunny spot.

I don't crave soil for sustenance
Or fancy irrigation.
I've got the perfect single life—
who needs cross-pollination?

But I am not your hardy mums
or dusty Boston greens.
Get one that settles, sinks its roots,
for your domestic scenes.

And I will hang around some more,
so free of earthy ties.
But looking down, I never see
what macramé belies.

The Inn:
The Florist

"Mom, where are my snowpants?" came the yell
from up the stairs. "I have to bring them in
today or else I lose a classroom point."
    "Me, too, me too, I lose a classroom point!"
"You do not, stupid, you don't go to school."
    "Do too, do too, Mom, tell her that I do!"
She took a breath and counted out again—
six hyacinths, six daffodils, two tulips—
"Mom!"—louder this time, definitely a scream—
"she PUSHED me!"
                "Damn it. Tom, can you go see…"
"The truck won't start, I'm out here getting cables."
    "I have to get the flowers to the inn
before the guests wake up." She went upstairs,
found snowpants, brushed two heads, poured cereal,
and counted in her head, "six hyacinths…."

When Tom and the kids had set off in the truck,
off to his folks' till she got them for school,
she ran back to the greenhouse, counting out
the rooms and then the pots, imagining
each grouping, with its scent and height and color.
She moved them to the van in trays of twenty
but brought the lily of the valley last—
white, delicate, and trembling, but the smell
could kill you with its happy, cloying sweetness.
She didn't want *that* filling up the van.
She took the icy driveway down the hill
and prayed the brakes held out. When she arrived,
Jed opened up the bay. "Here, let me help."

"You don't have to," she smiled.
                          "Oh, that's okay,
I know you have to get the kids to school."
They carried trays inside, she taking care
not to brush the sleeve of his flannel jacket.
She wheeled the loaded cart along the hallways,
placing one hyacinth on a spindly table,
a group of three—two lilies and one tulip—
on the sideboard in the upstairs sitting room.
A daffodil in the stairway to the lobby,
where Mrs. Armitage, who did the books
and knitted hats and mittens for the kids,
could see them— "nothing like a spot of yellow
to brighten up a January morning."
Carrying some roses to the lounge,
she sniffed the air—no coffee brewing yet—
then headed into the solarium,
glass-walled and facing south, the place she saved
for last. Quiet. Still dark. Her favorite time.
The flowers' faint breaths in the air—she knew
them all, cupping each bloom within her palm,
brushing her fingertips along their soil.
The amaryllis needed watering.

Playing Along

Florida, but Inland

I practiced pinball in the two-room clubhouse
at Hidden Lake the summer I was twelve.
We'd just moved to this complex east of town—
no lake, just asphalt and a laundry room.

I played alone until I met her—Shelley,
long hair, white-blond, which she wore loose, on purpose
(I didn't learn "tow-headed" until later).

She had a bike. Not a "bicycle," like mine—
a Schwinn, picked by my New York City parents,
who took me to a store where I was measured
for proper fit from saddle down to pedal—
but a "bike," from KMart, with a banana seat.

Shelley was bossy, also younger, but
she knew where we could ride to get a Slurpee,
the Seven-Eleven down Palm Avenue.
She told me about the Girls' Club as we passed,
which I thought was some kind of orphanage,
but with a pool, which made the girls seem lucky.
I wondered if she'd steal a candy bar
while we were there, or make me take a BlowPop;
instead she bought some gum—grape Bubbalicious,
something I was not allowed to have,
or so I thought. I bought some anyway.

On our way home, when I was turning into
the complex, left hand straight out, signaling,
I bumped a car's back fender with my tire.
I don't remember seeing her again
that summer—my own decision, I suppose,
to stay inside our air conditioned unit.
I'd never thought a girl might steal before.

SmartTales

Red Riding Hood

Let's say that you're partial to hoods,
and you're off to bring Grandma the goods—
those teeth are a hint,
be ready to sprint,
Verizon's one bar in these woods.

Cinderella

Let's say that you have a new dress,
and your boyfriend is anyone's guess:
go enjoy being posh
as long as your squash
has a clock and a good GPS.

Snow White

It's not smart when you're home all alone—
though an Apple is fine for a phone—
to take fruit that looks sweet
from a crone that you meet
while a battle is on for the throne.

Sleeping Beauty

Let's say that she's stuck in a castle
in a spell that is really quite facile.
Why fight the unseen—
can you kiss through a screen?
Use Zoom and avoid all the hassle.

The Beast Talks to Beauty

"Are you sick of being seen as a cutie,
though you've brains and a strong sense of duty?
While my looks tend to hinder
my chances on Tinder,
swipe right to see my inner Beauty."

Man of Steel

Lois is trapped by falling rocks? Go get her!
It's simple what we want from Superman—
to save the world (at least make bad things better).
The feats that we wish we could do? He can.

And yet he mostly follows natural laws.
Each superpower is just human strength
compounded—carbon fused with iron, flaws
like any alloy. He'll go to any length

to save the day, but he can't disappear.
His x-rays? Foiled by elemental lead.
He doesn't get the girl. Steeled but sincere,
our hero stutters on the phone instead.

We like him for how strong a man can be—
We love him for his flaws, ironically.

Russian "Trolls" Disrupt Elections

The sidewalk is filling with trolls—
the millennial version of moles,
they walk in to work,
there's no need to lurk,
no hiding behind grassy knolls.

They clearly all have the same mother.
Each one looks the same as the other.
They have stylized do's,
in greens, pinks, and blues,
and you (cough) can't tell sister from brother.

One troll enters and sits in his place,
starts his laptop and opens up Facebook. He's a "rancher from Texas"
and a "wife with a Lexus,"
and he's off to disrupt cyberspace.

Each morning he's given new goals.
He works at perfecting his roles—
going deep in the psyche
of Susie and Mikey,
by donning their virtual souls.

As Susie he buys crystal glasses
and has signed up for lots of new classes—
vegan cooking, pilates
(Mikey likes the taut bodies),
the opiate of these new masses.

His job is to skew the election—
there's a contest within every section.
If he gets the most friends,
he will win a new Benz
with bumper to bumper protection.

These days there are no Bolsheviks.
This isn't about politics
nor the news, true or fake,
just the dough he can make
from all those American clicks.

But as he makes each brand new friend,
Mikey/Susie can see a new trend.
Having friends feels fantastic—
he forgets that he's plastic,
and he moves to New York in the end.

Brooklyn Personals

Soy milk seeking coffee mate:
almond substitutes are great,
so are coconut or rice—
hemp would certainly suffice.
Fridge is tiny, bills are high,
only want one "milk" to buy—
half-and-half need not apply.

The Doctor and the Patient in the Next Exam Bay

"Sing it again," I want to ask them both
as I sit here alone behind mesh drapes
on paper drawn across a vinyl table—
easier to clean but somehow sticky,
not cold, instead uncomfortably warm,
as though I feel the heat of the last patients
(old man? sad woman?), as though they might be catching.

"Sing it again," I want to ask them both,
this patient and her doctor, reminiscing
about their old high school, a place I know
as run-down now, dingy and not the jewel
that they remember. She's in her seventies
(I overheard her birthdate earlier);
the doctor sounds younger, but not by much.

"Sing it again," I wish, when they are done.
It took me by surprise to hear them there,
talking about a neighborhood and then
singing—*Christos Anesti,* their favorite prayer.
It took me by surprise, in this fluorescent
light where I've been waiting—though not too long—
that people sometimes do burst into song.

Speed of Sound

Onstage at Carnegie, playing his sax,
did Charlie Parker ever think a woman
in a house deep in the woods
would sit in front of a fire
listening

70 years later
to his alto sax onstage at Carnegie,
the way that I imagine

you
sitting somewhere in the future,
having perhaps never heard of Parker
except through this,
leapfrogging back

to short quick trumpet blasts,
the ever-present mumble of the congas,
the sax a dancing dervish,

as the fire crackles
and the cat washes himself,
and the pen moves silently across the paper.

Playing Along in Temple

A basket of multi-colored egg shakers sits next to the prayer books at the entrance with the sign, "Please take one and play along as we sing."

The man who taps his egg to keep the beat,
not on the up beat, nothing syncopated,
just one after another, tap, tap, tap.

What is faith? That is faith.

The man who trips while walking to the *bimah,*
and doesn't see it as a metaphor.

What is faith? That is faith.

The man who sits and smiles as he sings,
his finger following along the text
though clearly he already knows the words.

What is faith? That is faith

or I'm imagining it all—
the faith, the fall, music, the man, the egg.

The Inn:
The Piano Player

The drive up here tonight was really bad.
Class finished early, but some kids were worried—
same conversation every year, for years.
I'm not supposed to grade on talent, but...
absurd. That's why they're here, to learn, improve,
then weed them out. They have to know by now
that's what it's all about. Well, that, and luck.

So I left late. The roads were bad, the snow
blinding. I do this drive three times a week,
and usually it's fine with four-wheel drive.
Tonight, gripping the wheel made my hands hurt.
It's getting tiring, these three long days,
but I still love that first glimpse of the inn
when I come over the mountain to the valley,
all lit up, warm and cozy, like a home.
I know there'll be a fire in the fireplace,
and someone leaves a rosebud on my piano.
Sometimes I'll pretend I'm Katharine Hepburn
in my white gown, those "house in a snowstorm" scenes
in every movie.
                I jump right in with "My Way."
I've got a rhythm here (no pun intended)—
pre-dinner cocktails are a certain crowd,
the kind of folks that like their Frank and Dean,
even though they're mostly boomer age.
That lasts about an hour, they leave for dinner,
and there's a little lull. I take a break—
Jed will usually have a plate and drink
ready for me, so I eat at the bar.
I'd like to have a drink at the piano,

but management thinks it gives the wrong impression,
(a dame long in the tooth sipping a drink
can easily appear a boozy lush).

The next wave is the parents of the babies,
lucky enough to have someone upstairs
who'll watch the kids while they cram in romance
before they fall asleep themselves, exhausted.
They're younger so I have to play Buble,
Grobin, the songs I pick up from my students.
After that the crowd's my age again,
so I can have some fun, veer into show tunes,
or jazz or classic rock or even country,
depending on the crowd. I like to sing
(the more they drink the better, I'm not that good).
It's better with a singer in the crowd—
I can spot them, I'll wave them to come up.
A few words back and forth—the song, the key—
and it's a stage, a movie. It feels good.
I usually go before it's closing time—
I leave the piano open for the guests.
As I walk toward the lobby, I sometimes hear
a few notes following me down the hall.

Reading the Signs

Reading the Signs

So-and-so slept here, a date, a list
of battles fought—whatever they're about,
he reads them all, not just to get the gist
but top to bottom, loudly, calling out
excitedly, *listen to this, you guys,*
to share with them this knowledge on display,
this one cool fact. The kids all roll their eyes—
there goes Dad again—and walk away.
They've tuned him out so often that I guess
he's background noise; they never catch the words,
he's like a soundtrack to their lives—no, less,
refrigerator hum, or maybe birds.
He keeps on reading—oblivious, content.
Maybe someday they'll know what he meant.

Cloud 9

Cloud 9 is always touted as
the perfect place to be.
But where's the place for things that are
less than heavenly?

The moderate joy of raisin bran,
a morning's smooth commute—
I'd only need Cloud 2 or 3
for puppies that are cute.

A 4 or 5 might do for coffee,
books that I have read.
Cloud 6 or 7's getting up there—
college degrees, fresh bread.

8, for me, would be the zenith—
babies, weddings too,
that's the cloud I'd use to show
the joy I feel with you.

Not that you don't deserve a 9,
it's just that, in my way,
I'd always keep 9 in reserve
for some impossible day.

And yet, one day, I'll take your hand,
one day, close to death,
I'll think "there's nothing else," and whisper
"9" with my last breath.

Funeral Potatoes

A Mormon dish called funeral potatoes,
ubiquitous and creamy, full of cheese,
appears at every family funeral—
no Mormon dies without a side of these.

They fill a spot on all the mourners' plates
next to the slaws and casseroles and meat,
and as the dead approach the Pearly Gates,
the living do their part—they sit and eat.

My question on this lumpy sustenance:
How did it start, as food or something more—
a humble symbol, earthly, blind, and dense,
a Mormon's not-so-gourmet metaphor?

Or maybe, it's that, any time of year,
potatoes are just what there was at hand,
rattling around a farmhouse bin somewhere
or scrabbled from the dusty promised land.

And just by dint of sheer dull repetition—
a funeral a month for years on end—
potatoes gained this deathly reputation;
what started as a meal became a trend.

Regardless, here they are, loaded with meaning:
"Someone you love just died." To make it through,
maybe a potato's what you need
to serve as comfort when no words will do.

Recipe for Disaster

The art of cooking isn't hard to master.
Read Julia, Beard, issues of *Food and Wine;*
Most likely it won't turn out a disaster.

Nowadays learn a new dish even faster—
with recipes shared everywhere online,
the art of cooking isn't hard to master.

But these were family secrets in the past, or
more personal, a woman's own design—
borrowing recipes could spell disaster.

Mistakes "crept in": the sugar, salt in vaster
quantities, a "4" rewritten "9"—
of course the art of cooking's hard to master

when following vague measurements, like "dash" or
"handful." Anything could undermine
the meal and make it turn out a disaster.

The author then would shrug and faintly gesture,
forcing her smile into a somber line:
"The art of cooking is so hard to master,
I'm sorry it all turned out a disaster."

Planning Ahead

Curtains for me—pale yellow, no, light blue—,
couches where I can sit with company,
bright pillows, open windows, and a few
blankets against a chill, placed casually.
We'll have good music: Mozart, Mendelsohn,
all kinds of jazz— "At Last" and "In the Mood"—
and dancing—Elvis, Michael, Ellington.
Great poetry to read aloud, and food:
chocolate, lovely, dark and deep; and sushi;
across the room, a bar. I must remember
peaches (note to self—to have them juicy,
it's best for this to happen in September).
But there's the rub: I've planned out how to die—
I haven't planned (so far) the when and why.

Heading Out

I should stop kissing you goodbye.
It's not a sign of love,
but fear that while I'm out you'll die,
and then I think, what of?

I worry most about disease—
each week a different kind.
Today I cannot find my keys—
Alzheimer's comes to mind.

"That can't kick in," you kindly say,
"in the hours you'll be gone.
So go, have fun, enjoy the day,
I plan to mow the lawn."

Mowing? Images fill my head—
a stroke, a heart attack.
You groan, "I'm fine, and if I'm dead,
no need to hurry back."

"Okay, I'm leaving, back at four."
"I love you," you reply.
How sweet, I think, hand on the door,
I should kiss you goodbye.

Dressed for the Party

for Ryan (1985–2015)

Your ruffled shirt is what I noticed first
at your mom's birthday party. We conversed,
and you were quite the gentleman, to flirt
harmlessly with your mother's friend, alert
the bartender to fill my glass. You nursed

your ginger ale, decanted wine, dispersed
the waiters with one gesture, and, well-versed
at being host, you served us all dessert
in your ruffled shirt.

The boy in you, though, teased, snuck up and burst
balloons and laughed. Your brown eyes held your thirst
for fun, for dares, for playing in the dirt;
skinned knees; bruised heart; and other kinds of hurt
to come—your only shield against the worst,
your ruffled shirt.

Tomato Seedlings in the Window

Green eyebrows,
winking,
look—we did it again,
we grew,
without any help
from you, no matter
what you were thinking.

True, water, this crumbly medium—
now go away,
leave us to the
tedium of rebirth,
growth, the alchemy
of turning air and heat to destiny.

Somewhere in our future
are thickened stalks,
gnarled, bent over with the weight
of waiting

but now we are gossamer,
translucent, thready,
we are green,
the only green,
heady, almost obscene
when all around
is blasted brown
and gray—

we bow down sunward,
the time is nearing,
winter is riven,
we grab what we are given.

The Inn:
The Bartender

I

"An Aviation? Sure, I can make that.
Yes, Bombay gin. Yep, crème de violette.
Yes, Pete will bring it over when it's ready."
His smiled never wavered as he talked.
After the man went to his table, Jed
took down two cocktail glasses from the rack,
placing them on the polished bar. He turned
to the array of gleaming liquor bottles
along the mirrored wall, selected three.
The clink of ice against the metal shaker,
the quick sharp pours into the measured glass,
the crackle of the ice. The shake, the strain.
Two sweating cocktails glimmered in the light.
A nod to Pete, who took them on a tray.
A slight tug on his vest, then turning to
a couple at the bar. "Another beer?"
he asked the man.
      "No thanks, not yet."
                              His hands
went to the towel tucked into his waistband,
and he returned to polishing the glasses.

II

Five minutes later, he checked in again.
"How did you like the cocktail? Sweet enough?"
he asked the woman.
        "Yes!"
              "I thought you would.

Manhattans are too bitter. These are sweeter."
The man nodded and gestured at his beer.
Jed filled the pint glass. "Where are you folks from?"
   "New Hampshire," she replied. "And you live here?
   You ski?"
                      "I do, but mostly I'm at work—
I run the restaurant right on the slope,
the one that's at the top of Devil's Run."
   "Then you come here at night? That's a long day."

The Aviation gestured, sharp, impatient,
and Jed pulled glasses down and made the refill.
"That ever bug you?" asked the man. "Would me."
Jed shrugged. "They're not so bad, and they tip well.
Sometimes they can't see who's in front of them.
I'm saving for my own place, pub and bar.
Be my own boss, doing what I love.
I've lived here all my life. It's finally time."
His fingers brushed the flower in his lapel.

Contours

Contours

canyon
deep, jagged
the shape of water

rock
tall, rounded
the shape of wind

everything
is the shape
of something
gone by

canyon, water
rock, wind

absence
the shape left behind

Prop Tools

My friend the carpenter (no, not *that* one)
Told me about a trick some workmen use.
They leave some tools around if they're not done—
Nothing that they can't afford to lose—

As if they've gone for coffee or a snack
Or an emergency—a roof with leaks.
They want to keep us thinking, "They'll be back,"
Despite the fact that days stretch into weeks.

But even if they do this to deceive,
They do it. They need us to think that they're
Decent, the kind of men who wouldn't leave.
That Skilsaw on the ground shows wear and tear,
A lot like faith. We need it. So do they.
A promise to believe in anyway.

The March of Time

My heart begins to race (in turtle time)
watching him lumber closer, a slow pace
more nerve-wracking than speed. This birthday I'm
relaxing here and trying not to trace
the march of time. I watch him lift a foot—
I think I could go make a cup of tea
in all the time it takes for him to put
it down again. And now he's watching me.

There must be something that seems slow to turtles—
the way I wait for each blink endlessly—
rock-time, evolutionary hurdles,
marvels I live too fast to even see.
But me with my, he with his turtled eye,
we watch the same infinities blink by.

Arroyo

It's a dry year this year. In the arroyo
the sheep jostle their way down steep banks, low
—lower down than last year, thinks Ramirez—
to find water. He notices the mark
of last year's flood high up the sides. They trot
faster as they get closer—he hears the bell

of the sure-footed ram in front, the bell-
wether of the flock who owns the arroyo—
at least among the sheep, who clump and trot
behind. Arriving, the ram lets out a bellow—
a bleat being the sound of panic, a mark
of fear, and he fears nothing. At least Ramirez

thinks the ram fears nothing. Not like Ramirez,
who each day fears the clanging of the bell,
the gravelly rumble, snort, and roar that mark
a flood's rapid approach in the arroyo.
But no rain's coming and the water's low.
He should get a dog, he thinks, who'd trot

easily down the slope and make them trot
to safety with him. Evenings, as Ramirez
strolls through town relaxing, his dog would follow.
He likes the city—people, the church's bell
pealing, grand buildings. Not like the arroyo—
remote and dull, the opposite of landmark,

the place is an aside, a snide remark
in this translation of a life, a trot
instead of the real story. *The arroyo*
is burying the man who is Ramirez.
He likes this gloomy metaphor, the bell
tolling for him, he thinks, deep and low.

He stops outside the 7-11, low
on cigarettes. The dog would circle, mark
his territory, waiting for the bell
above the door that says it's time to trot
alongside this remarkable Ramirez,
lead the way back to the dry arroyo

that could flood at any moment, and trot
below high-water marks to guard Ramirez
from sheep, from bells, from flood and the arroyo.

The Molt

I am not the creature but the shell.
I am not hiding but the space to hide,
the sturdy walls around a place to dwell.

At first my structure is a citadel—
the creature's safest when it stays inside.
I am not the creature but the shell,

yet as the creature grows, its needs compel
a sloughing off—my flaws are magnified.
My sturdy walls surround a place to dwell

but trapped inside this small a space is hell.
The creature leaves. The shell's unoccupied.
I am not the creature but the shell,

useless as when the clapper leaves the bell,
water the well. With nothing to provide,
my walls surround an empty place. I dwell

on spiraling echoes of nothing left to tell,
of no one left who ever laughed or cried.
I am not the creature but the shell,
the sturdy walls around a place to dwell.

The Inn:
The Baker

Alarm is set for 4.
                    It was our dream.
We'd move up here when we retired—a farmhouse,
small, where she and I could garden, write.
The kids would come to visit, send the grandkids.
A porch where we could sit and watch the mountains.
All fine, then 9 months in, she found the lump.
So yeah.

      I wandered through the house for weeks,
just touching things. The kids came up. They tried
to help. I sent them home, with promises.

I figured I could start with something easy—
her cookbooks. Not my thing, I could get rid
of those. I pulled the first one off the shelf.
Sat down—there on the cover was the challah
she'd bake for holidays, nice dinners, or the kids.
The book fell open to the page, flour-splotched,
wrinkled—she always did make such a mess.
I never baked stuff. I was on the grill—
steaks, burgers—or lasagna for the kids.
But as I read the steps, I thought perhaps
I'd try. I finally found the yeast (the fridge),
the rest was pretty easy: flour, salt,
sugar, water, eggs. It was the kneading
I liked—the working, working, then the feel
of—I don't know. The dough felt warm, alive.
I left it rising in a bowl, was thrilled
(yes, me, the big attorney, actually thrilled)
to come back later, see how it had grown.
The gust of breath when I just punched it down.

The rising up again against that punch
and then the baking, and it turned to bread
(I know, what else, and yet, actual bread!).
I tore a hunk (she'd never let me do that)
and ate it, leaning up against the counter.

I figured, why not, branched out, made her pinwheels,
some rolls, and then a sachertorte we'd had
on some vacation once. I heard her voice
(I missed her, but I didn't miss her nagging!)
telling me to watch my weight, clean up,
give some to the neighbors—they had kids.

So when I saw the sign for bakers needed,
I took some bread and cake down to the inn.
They wanted some experience, but I
convinced them that they should give me a chance
(at least my legal skills were good for something—
it didn't hurt that they were desperate).

Now I get up at 4, head to the inn,
make myself a coffee and get started.
I like the moment every morning when
the dough begins to live beneath my hands.
The smell of fresh-baked cookies, big and warm,
the kids whose eyes are round like chocolate chips,
waiting for me to wrap it in wax paper
(ignoring their fingerprints on the glass case),
hand it straight to them and make their day.
Jeez, who's talking here, is this still me?

I like it. It's not fascinating, but
at least it gets me out of bed. It's good.
Maybe not forever but for now.

Echoes

"Do the kitchen? I'll give you Swedish Fish!"
I hear negotiations reach a peak,
numbers flying, the clatter of each dish—
the kids are home, visiting for the week.

That gummy currency bought lots of things—
a chore, "shotgun," a TV show, a wish.
It's less like cash and more like sonar pings,
locating love that could be found with Fish.

Adults now, pairing Fish with cabernet,
they tease and trade and get the kitchen done.
It's like old times, and then they go away,
as we adjust to plus or minus one.

Everything's clean, back in its place, or mostly.
And still I hear the sound of fish, but ghostly.

About the Author

Midge Goldberg has published two previous books of poems, *Snowman's Code* and *Flume Ride*. She was the recipient of the Richard Wilbur Poetry Award and the Howard Nemerov Sonnet Award and has been published in numerous journals and anthologies. In addition, she is the author of the children's book *My Best Ever Grandpa*. She received a B.A. from Yale University and an MFA from the University of New Hampshire. She lives in Chester, N.H., with her husband, the poet Robert W. Crawford.

www.ingramcontent.com/pod-product-compliance
Lightning Source LLC
Chambersburg PA
CBHW020730100426
42735CB00038B/1662